PRINCEWILL LAGANG

Agriculture in the Digital Age: Entrepreneurship in Farming

First published by PRINCEWILL LAGANG 2023

Copyright © 2023 by Princewill Lagang

All rights reserved. No part of this publication may be reproduced, stored or transmitted in any form or by any means, electronic, mechanical, photocopying, recording, scanning, or otherwise without written permission from the publisher. It is illegal to copy this book, post it to a website, or distribute it by any other means without permission.

Princewill Lagang asserts the moral right to be identified as the author of this work.

First edition

This book was professionally typeset on Reedsy.
Find out more at reedsy.com

Contents

1. Agriculture in the Digital Age: Entrepreneurship in Farming — 1
2. Digital Seeds of Change: The Rise of Precision Agriculture — 4
3. Cultivating Sustainability: Agriculture's Environmental... — 7
4. The Digital Farmer: Navigating Challenges and Opportunities — 10
5. From Farm to Fork: The Digital Revolution in Food... — 13
6. Agriculture and the Digital Age: Challenges, Ethical... — 16
7. Seeds of Tomorrow: Education and Innovation in Agricultural... — 19
8. Nurturing Resilience: Agriculture's Role in a Changing World — 22
9. Harvesting the Future: Reflections on Agriculture in the... — 25
10. A Digital Harvest: Looking to the Future of Agriculture — 28
11. Cultivating a Shared Vision: Agriculture's Role in Global... — 31
12. The Human Element: Nurturing the Soul of Agriculture — 34
13. Summary — 37

1

Agriculture in the Digital Age: Entrepreneurship in Farming

The sun hung low in the early morning sky, casting a warm, golden glow across the vast expanse of rolling farmland. As the dew-kissed leaves glistened in the first light of day, a new chapter in the world of agriculture was unfolding. This chapter, like the chapters before it, was marked by innovation, adaptation, and the relentless pursuit of progress. Yet, in the digital age, the story of farming was being rewritten in ways never before imagined.

Agriculture, the cornerstone of human civilization, has come a long way since the dawn of time. From the earliest days of sowing seeds and tending livestock, to the industrial revolutions that transformed farms into efficient, mechanized operations, the evolution of agriculture has been a testament to human ingenuity. Today, as we stand on the precipice of a new era, the fusion of technology and farming is reshaping the agricultural landscape in profound ways.

The digital age has ushered in a wave of change across all sectors, and agriculture is no exception. It has given rise to a new breed of farmer, one who harnesses the power of data, automation, and connectivity to optimize their operations. These modern agricultural entrepreneurs understand that success in farming is no longer solely dependent on the whims of weather or the uncertainties of market fluctuations. Instead, they leverage the tools of the digital age to mitigate risks, increase productivity, and foster sustainability.

In this chapter, we embark on a journey to explore the transformation of agriculture through the lens of entrepreneurship. We delve into the stories of visionary farmers, forward-thinking startups, and agricultural enterprises that have harnessed technology to drive innovation. Through their experiences, we witness the challenges and opportunities that lie at the intersection of agriculture and the digital age.

The rural landscape is no longer disconnected from the world; it's a hub of connectivity and communication. The farmsteads and pastures are no longer just places of labor, but data-driven hubs where every aspect of the farming process is optimized for efficiency and sustainability. From precision agriculture techniques that enable farmers to make real-time decisions based on soil and weather data, to the use of drones and satellite imagery for crop monitoring and pest control, technology has become an indispensable tool in modern farming.

One of the central themes of this exploration is the idea of entrepreneurship within farming. The modern farmer is not just a producer of food; they are a problem solver, a risk-taker, and a business innovator. We delve into the stories of farmers who have not only embraced technology but also developed new revenue streams by diversifying their agricultural ventures. Whether it's agritourism, value-added products, or direct-to-consumer sales, these entrepreneurial farmers are finding innovative ways to sustain and grow their businesses in the digital age.

But this transformation is not without its challenges. The digital age has brought with it new questions and concerns, from data privacy and security to the potential digital divide in rural areas. As we explore the ever-evolving landscape of agriculture, we also consider the ethical, social, and economic implications of this digital revolution.

In the pages that follow, we will meet the pioneers who are redefining what it means to be a farmer in the 21st century. We will uncover the strategies, technologies, and philosophies that drive their success, and we will confront the complex issues that arise as agriculture and entrepreneurship intersect in the digital age. Together, we will embark on a journey through the heartlands and fields, where the roots of tradition intertwine with the branches of innovation, shaping the future of farming and food production.

2

Digital Seeds of Change: The Rise of Precision Agriculture

As the sun ascended higher in the sky, casting its midday warmth upon the fields, our journey into the digital age of farming continued. In this chapter, we delve into the heart of the technological revolution sweeping across agriculture, a revolution known as precision agriculture. Here, we uncover how modern farmers are using data, sensors, and automation to cultivate their fields with unprecedented accuracy, efficiency, and sustainability.

Precision agriculture, often referred to as precision farming or smart farming, is the practice of using advanced technologies to optimize various aspects of the farming process. It's a practice that brings the principles of science, engineering, and data analytics to the age-old art of farming. The goal is simple: to do more with less, to maximize yields while minimizing inputs, and to farm in a way that's not only economically viable but also environmentally responsible.

At the heart of precision agriculture lies the notion that every inch of a field is unique, and it should be treated as such. Gone are the days of applying the same amount of water, fertilizer, or pesticides uniformly across an entire field. Instead, modern farmers use a combination of GPS, remote sensing, and data analysis to create maps of their fields that detail variations in soil composition, moisture levels, and crop health. Armed with this data, they can precisely tailor their actions to suit the specific needs of each area, resulting in optimized resource usage and increased productivity.

One of the key tools in the precision agriculture toolkit is the Global Positioning System (GPS). GPS technology allows farmers to precisely map their fields, track the movement of machinery, and record data with remarkable accuracy. Tractors and other farm equipment are often equipped with GPS receivers and automated steering systems, allowing for straighter rows, reduced overlap, and less soil compaction.

Moreover, drones have become invaluable in agriculture. These aerial vehicles are equipped with cameras and sensors that can capture high-resolution images and data, providing farmers with real-time information about crop health, pest infestations, and even irrigation needs. The use of drones not only saves time but also enables early intervention, preventing crop losses and reducing the need for chemical treatments.

Sensors are another cornerstone of precision agriculture. These small, smart devices can be embedded in the soil, attached to plants, or placed on equipment. They collect data on everything from soil moisture and temperature to nutrient levels and crop growth, all of which is transmitted wirelessly to a central data hub. Farmers can then monitor this information remotely and make timely decisions.

Big data analytics play a critical role in making sense of the vast amount of data collected on the farm. Farmers can use powerful software and machine learning algorithms to gain insights into historical trends, predict future outcomes, and make data-driven decisions. For example, they can forecast the best time to plant, the most suitable irrigation schedule, and the optimal harvesting window, all based on data analysis.

In this chapter, we will meet farmers who have embraced precision agriculture and learn from their experiences. We will explore the technological marvels that have revolutionized farming practices and discuss the environmental benefits of reduced input use. We will also dive into the challenges and limitations of precision agriculture, from the cost of implementing technology to data security concerns.

As we turn the digital pages of this chapter, we discover that precision agriculture is not just a technological advancement; it's a philosophy that seeks to redefine the relationship between the farmer, the land, and the food we all depend on. It is a chapter in the ongoing story of agriculture where innovation meets sustainability, and the potential for growth is as boundless as the fertile fields that stretch before us.

3

Cultivating Sustainability: Agriculture's Environmental Imperative

As the day progressed, our exploration of the changing landscape of agriculture led us to a critical chapter in the story of farming in the digital age: sustainability. In this chapter, we will delve into the profound impact that technology and innovative farming practices have on the environment, and how the agricultural community is responding to the urgent call for a more sustainable and regenerative approach to food production.

The environmental challenges facing agriculture today are both daunting and pressing. Climate change, loss of biodiversity, soil degradation, water scarcity, and pollution all pose significant threats to the future of farming. The need for more sustainable agricultural practices has never been more evident. Fortunately, the digital age is providing the tools and solutions to address these challenges.

One of the central themes of this chapter is the adoption of sustainable farming practices, from no-till and conservation tillage to cover cropping and crop rotation. These techniques reduce soil erosion, enhance soil health, and sequester carbon. With the help of digital tools, farmers can better manage these practices and measure their impact over time, allowing for continuous improvement.

Digital platforms and data-driven decision-making play a crucial role in sustainable agriculture. Farmers can monitor soil quality, weather patterns, and water usage to optimize resource allocation and reduce waste. This not only increases farm efficiency but also lessens the environmental footprint of each operation.

Furthermore, precision agriculture, which we explored in the previous chapter, is inherently tied to sustainability. By precisely applying inputs such as water, fertilizers, and pesticides, farmers can reduce the overuse of these resources, leading to more efficient and environmentally friendly farming.

Sustainable agriculture is not limited to land-based farming. Aquaculture, hydroponics, and vertical farming are gaining traction as innovative approaches to produce food sustainably. These methods use technology to minimize water usage, reduce land requirements, and optimize nutrient delivery, all while producing food close to urban centers, reducing the carbon footprint associated with transportation.

The use of renewable energy sources such as solar panels and wind turbines is becoming increasingly common on farms. This not only reduces the energy costs of farming but also contributes to a more sustainable energy mix.

In this chapter, we will meet farmers and innovators who have made sustainability a core part of their agricultural mission. We will explore regenerative farming practices, the importance of biodiversity in food production, and the role of organic and agroecological farming in building a more sustainable food system.

We will also examine the complex relationship between agriculture and climate change. How can agriculture mitigate its own contribution to greenhouse gas emissions? How can it adapt to the changing climate and contribute to climate resilience? These questions are at the forefront of discussions in the digital age of farming.

As we journey through this chapter, we come to understand that sustainability in agriculture is not just a buzzword or a trend; it's an imperative. It's a recognition that the land, water, and air upon which farming depends are finite resources that must be carefully stewarded for the well-being of current and future generations. Sustainability is the bridge that connects technology, innovation, and the environment in a quest to ensure that the world's growing population can be fed while also protecting the planet's natural resources.

4

The Digital Farmer: Navigating Challenges and Opportunities

The sun began its descent toward the horizon, casting long shadows over the landscape, and in this changing light, we turn our focus to the heart of the digital age of farming—the farmers themselves. In this chapter, we explore the transformative role that farmers play in shaping the future of agriculture, how they navigate the challenges and opportunities presented by technology, and the evolving identity of the "digital farmer."

The digital age has brought about profound changes in the lives of those who till the soil and tend to the land. Farmers have become stewards of data, utilizing technology to make informed decisions, manage resources, and optimize their operations. The traditional image of a farmer has evolved to include not only a deep understanding of agriculture but also a proficiency in data analysis, software use, and technology integration.

At the heart of this transformation is the concept of the "digital farmer," a term that encompasses those who embrace technology and innovation as essential tools in their agricultural endeavors. These individuals are not only cultivators of crops and caretakers of livestock but also data-driven decision-makers, sustainability advocates, and entrepreneurs.

The digital farmer's toolkit is vast and continually expanding. From smartphones and tablets used to access real-time data and manage farm operations remotely, to smart sensors and drones, the digital farmer relies on a diverse set of technologies to enhance productivity and sustainability.

This chapter introduces us to a cast of farmers from diverse backgrounds and regions who have adopted digital farming practices. We will hear their stories, discover the challenges they face, and learn from their experiences in integrating technology into their daily routines. Some of these farmers are the latest in a long line of agricultural traditions, while others are newcomers who have embraced farming as a second career or as a way to connect with their rural roots.

As the digital age intersects with agriculture, we explore the profound impact on rural communities. Technology has the potential to rejuvenate and revitalize rural areas by creating jobs in agtech, reducing the isolation that can come with farming, and opening new economic opportunities beyond traditional farming.

However, it's not all smooth sailing for the digital farmer. Challenges related to access to technology, data privacy, and the rapid pace of change in the agricultural tech landscape are ever-present. This chapter will delve into these challenges and how they can be overcome.

Moreover, the digital age has given rise to new ethical and social questions in agriculture. The collection of vast amounts of data, the role of multinational corporations in shaping agricultural technology, and the need for data security and privacy are subjects that require careful consideration.

The digital farmer is at the nexus of tradition and innovation, sustainability and profitability, and community and global connectivity. Their stories illuminate the complex and dynamic nature of modern agriculture, demonstrating that the digital age is not a threat to the farmer's way of life but a transformative force that can empower them to meet the challenges of a rapidly changing world.

As we turn the digital pages of this chapter, we gain insight into the evolving identity of the digital farmer, who stands as a beacon of hope and inspiration for the future of agriculture. They are not just the keepers of the land; they are the architects of a sustainable and thriving future for food production and the communities they serve.

5

From Farm to Fork: The Digital Revolution in Food Distribution

As the sun dipped below the horizon, signaling the end of another day in the agricultural world, our journey through the digital age of farming continued. In this chapter, we transition our focus from the fields and farms to the final destination of agricultural produce—the consumer's plate. Here, we explore how technology is revolutionizing the way food is distributed, connecting farmers and consumers in new and innovative ways.

Food distribution has always been a crucial but often overlooked aspect of the food system. From the moment a crop is harvested or an animal is processed, to the point it reaches the grocery store or restaurant, a complex web of logistics, transportation, and supply chain management is at play. The digital age has disrupted this system, offering opportunities for increased transparency, efficiency, and sustainability.

One of the transformative forces in food distribution is e-commerce. Online marketplaces and direct-to-consumer sales have empowered farmers and food producers to reach consumers without the need for traditional intermediaries. This shift not only benefits producers by allowing them to capture a larger share of the retail price but also offers consumers access to a wider variety of products and the ability to make informed choices about their food.

Farmers' markets, community-supported agriculture (CSA) programs, and online platforms have all facilitated this direct connection between producers and consumers. The digital age has enabled farmers to create virtual storefronts, offer home delivery, and provide detailed information about their products, including their production methods, farm practices, and even the stories behind their food.

On the other side of the spectrum, large-scale food distribution has also been reshaped by technology. The use of sensors, blockchain technology, and data analytics is enabling companies to monitor the temperature, humidity, and freshness of food products in real time during transportation, helping to reduce food waste and ensure food safety.

Additionally, artificial intelligence and machine learning are used to predict consumer demand, optimize inventory, and streamline the distribution process. These technologies are helping to ensure that food reaches consumers more efficiently, minimizing the environmental impact associated with long transportation routes and reducing the risk of food spoilage.

This chapter will introduce us to the digital disruptors in the food distribution space, from startups that connect consumers with local producers to tech giants that are redefining the supply chain. We will explore the challenges and opportunities that come with this transformation, including concerns about data privacy, the need for food safety and traceability, and the potential for rural revitalization.

We will also discuss the impact of the digital age on consumer behavior. Today's consumers are more conscious of where their food comes from, how it's produced, and its impact on the environment. Technology has provided the means for consumers to access this information, make informed choices, and even engage in a dialogue with the producers themselves.

In the final sections of this chapter, we will explore the potential for a more sustainable, local, and transparent food system, where digital technology connects every step in the supply chain, from farm to fork. The digital revolution in food distribution is reshaping the way we think about food and our connection to the people and places that produce it, ultimately driving us toward a more sustainable and informed food future.

6

Agriculture and the Digital Age: Challenges, Ethical Dilemmas, and the Path Forward

As the final traces of daylight faded, our exploration of agriculture in the digital age approached its conclusion. In this chapter, we confront the challenges, ethical dilemmas, and complex issues that arise as technology continues to reshape the agricultural landscape. We also look toward the path forward, seeking solutions and strategies for a sustainable, ethical, and inclusive digital agricultural future.

The digital age has brought tremendous benefits to agriculture, enhancing productivity, sustainability, and economic viability. However, it has also introduced a host of challenges and ethical dilemmas that demand our attention.

One of the foremost challenges is the digital divide. While technology holds the potential to empower farmers and rural communities, it also exacerbates disparities between those who have access to resources and those who do not. The lack of broadband internet in many rural areas hinders farmers from fully embracing digital tools and participating in the global agricultural market.

Data privacy and security have become pressing concerns in the digital age. The collection, storage, and use of agricultural data raise questions about who owns the data, who controls access, and how it can be exploited. The risk of data breaches, cyberattacks, and misuse of sensitive information adds complexity to the digital transformation of agriculture.

Another ethical dilemma revolves around the concentration of power and control in the hands of a few tech giants. Companies that provide digital farming solutions often hold immense influence over the industry, from the platforms used to the data collected. This concentration of power raises concerns about competition, fairness, and access to information and tools.

The environmental impact of technology in agriculture is a double-edged sword. While precision agriculture can reduce inputs and minimize environmental harm, the manufacturing and disposal of tech products, as well as energy consumption, are also a concern. Balancing these trade-offs is a delicate task.

Food safety and traceability are essential aspects of the digital food system. While technology can enhance food safety by tracking the movement of food products, it also amplifies the risks associated with contamination and the spread of foodborne illnesses. Ensuring the integrity of digital food systems is paramount.

In this chapter, we delve into the strategies and solutions aimed at addressing these challenges and dilemmas. From initiatives to bridge the digital divide and expand rural broadband access to the development of regulations and standards for data privacy and security, the path forward is multifaceted.

A key theme in this chapter is the role of ethical decision-making in the digital age of agriculture. Farmers, agtech companies, policymakers, and consumers all play a role in shaping the ethical landscape of agriculture. We explore how transparency, accountability, and responsible innovation can guide the integration of technology in farming.

The future of agriculture in the digital age is not predetermined; it is shaped by the collective actions and choices of the agricultural community, the tech industry, and society as a whole. By acknowledging the challenges and ethical dilemmas, we can work together to create an agricultural future that harnesses the potential of technology while preserving the values and principles that sustain the land, the people, and the communities that rely on it.

In the final section of this chapter, we reflect on the interplay of tradition and innovation, sustainability and productivity, and ethics and economics. It is through this dialogue and engagement that we find the path forward in agriculture's digital age, where technology and human values merge to build a more resilient, equitable, and prosperous future for all.

7

Seeds of Tomorrow: Education and Innovation in Agricultural Technology

As the first rays of dawn broke over the horizon, we arrived at the final chapter of our journey through the digital age of agriculture. In this chapter, we explore the critical role of education, innovation, and research in propelling the agricultural sector into a brighter, more sustainable future.

The integration of technology into agriculture has necessitated a workforce skilled in both traditional farming practices and cutting-edge digital tools. This chapter is a celebration of those who have taken it upon themselves to educate the next generation of farmers, researchers, and innovators.

Agricultural education has evolved to embrace the digital age, offering students opportunities to learn not only about the age-old traditions of farming but also about the latest advances in technology and data-driven decision-making. From agricultural colleges and universities to vocational programs and online courses, there are numerous pathways for individuals to gain the knowledge and skills required to thrive in modern agriculture.

Innovators in the field of agriculture are continuously pushing the boundaries of what is possible. This chapter showcases the work of scientists, engineers, and entrepreneurs who are developing cutting-edge technologies that promise to revolutionize the industry. From advanced robotics that can pick fruit with precision to gene editing techniques that hold the potential to create more resilient and nutritious crops, innovation is driving progress.

Research plays a central role in shaping the future of agriculture. We explore the work of agricultural scientists and their efforts to develop new crop varieties, improve pest and disease management, and enhance soil health. This research not only addresses the immediate challenges of agriculture but also contributes to long-term sustainability and food security.

One of the central themes of this chapter is the intersection of agriculture and the tech industry. Agtech startups are leveraging the power of digital technology to create solutions for farmers, from software that helps manage farm operations to hardware like autonomous tractors and drones. These companies are driving innovation and competition in the sector, empowering farmers to make more informed decisions and optimize their operations.

In addition to highlighting the achievements in agricultural technology, we also discuss the role of government and policy in supporting research and innovation in agriculture. Through grants, funding, and regulation, governments play a pivotal role in shaping the direction of agricultural technology.

The chapter concludes with a reflection on the importance of fostering a culture of innovation and collaboration within the agricultural community. It emphasizes the significance of cross-sector partnerships, where traditional farmers, researchers, technology experts, and policymakers work together to ensure that technology serves the needs of agriculture and society as a whole.

In the dawn of this new age of agriculture, the focus is not solely on productivity and profit but also on ethics, sustainability, and the preservation of the land. It is a vision of agriculture that cherishes tradition while embracing innovation, where education, innovation, and research are the driving forces that steer the sector toward a more prosperous and sustainable future.

As we bring this journey through the digital age of agriculture to a close, we find ourselves standing at the crossroads of tradition and innovation, where the seeds of tomorrow are sown by those who are committed to nurturing the land, advancing technology, and securing a resilient future for agriculture.

8

Nurturing Resilience: Agriculture's Role in a Changing World

The landscape was bathed in the soft, golden light of early morning as we ventured into the final chapter of our exploration of agriculture in the digital age. In this chapter, we delve into the multifaceted challenges that the agricultural sector faces in an ever-changing world and examine its role in building resilience for the future.

As the world grapples with climate change, shifting demographics, and increasing global connectivity, agriculture stands at the forefront of both the challenges and solutions. In this chapter, we scrutinize how the digital age has enabled agriculture to adapt and contribute to a more sustainable and resilient future.

One of the central themes of this chapter is climate change and its impact on agriculture. We explore how shifting weather patterns, more frequent extreme events, and changing growing seasons have forced farmers to adapt and innovate. Technology, from precision agriculture to climate modeling, has been instrumental in helping farmers make informed decisions in the face of uncertainty.

In a world where the global population continues to grow, agriculture faces the monumental task of producing more food while minimizing its environmental impact. We delve into the concept of sustainable intensification, where farmers strive to maximize productivity on existing land while minimizing resource use, and how technology is a driving force behind this effort.

The digital age has also opened up opportunities for farmers to diversify their income streams. We examine how agritourism, value-added products, and direct-to-consumer sales have become viable options for agricultural entrepreneurs. These strategies not only help increase farmers' resilience but also strengthen the connection between producers and consumers.

In this chapter, we address the social and economic dimensions of resilience in agriculture. From the importance of rural development and revitalization to the need for inclusive, equitable systems that ensure access to technology and opportunities for all, we explore how the agricultural sector can contribute to a more just and resilient society.

The role of data and information in building resilience cannot be overstated. From early warning systems for pest outbreaks and extreme weather events to the use of blockchain technology to trace the origin of food products, the digital age has provided tools for ensuring the integrity and reliability of the agricultural supply chain.

We also look at the global dimension of resilience in agriculture, exploring how international cooperation, research, and trade can help ensure food security in a changing world. As the challenges facing agriculture know no borders, it is imperative that nations work together to address them.

The final pages of this chapter underscore the importance of the human element in building resilience. Farmers, researchers, policymakers, and consumers all play a role in shaping the future of agriculture. The story of agriculture in the digital age is ultimately a story of resilience, of human ingenuity and determination in the face of a changing world.

As we conclude our journey through the digital age of agriculture, we leave behind a legacy of innovation, adaptation, and hope. The digital age has ushered in a new era for agriculture, one where technology and tradition, sustainability and productivity, and resilience and opportunity converge to shape a more resilient and prosperous future for the agricultural sector and the global community it sustains.

9

Harvesting the Future: Reflections on Agriculture in the Digital Age

As the sun painted the sky in hues of orange and purple, we found ourselves at the end of our journey through the digital age of agriculture. In this final chapter, we reflect on the profound transformations, the enduring values, and the boundless possibilities that this age has brought to the world of farming and food production.

Our exploration has taken us through the fields of innovation, sustainability, education, and resilience in agriculture, but it is in the reflection on these journeys that we uncover the essence of what agriculture means in the digital age.

The digital age has redefined the role of the farmer. No longer confined to the image of toiling the land with just their hands, today's farmer is a knowledge worker, a data analyst, and a technology user. Farmers are embracing innovation, adapting to change, and leading the charge in developing sustainable practices. They are the custodians of the land, stewards of tradition, and architects of a more resilient future.

The digital age has given rise to the concept of "smart farming," where data and technology combine to optimize every aspect of agriculture. From the precision application of inputs to the use of automation and robotics, farming is becoming more efficient, productive, and environmentally friendly. Smart farming holds the potential to meet the growing demand for food while conserving resources and protecting the environment.

Sustainability is not just a buzzword; it's a core principle in the digital age of agriculture. We've seen how sustainable farming practices, supported by technology and innovation, can reduce the environmental footprint of agriculture. The soil, water, and air that are vital for agriculture's survival are being safeguarded, ensuring that future generations will have the same opportunities.

Education and innovation have been instrumental in this transformation. Agricultural education has evolved to prepare the next generation for the demands of modern farming, where data analysis, technology integration, and entrepreneurship are as important as plowing a field. Innovators, researchers, and entrepreneurs have created a dynamic landscape where new technologies, products, and solutions are constantly emerging to address the challenges of agriculture.

The challenges and ethical dilemmas we've encountered in this journey have been a reminder that the digital age is not without its complexities. From data privacy to the digital divide, concentration of power to the environmental impact of technology, we have grappled with questions that demand our attention and action.

In the midst of these challenges, we have discovered the resilience of agriculture. Farmers have faced adversity for centuries, and the digital age has only strengthened their capacity to adapt and innovate. It is a reminder that the essence of agriculture lies not just in the production of food but in the people who tend the land and in the communities that rely on it.

This journey has revealed the interplay of tradition and innovation, sustainability and productivity, ethics and economics. The digital age of agriculture is a testament to the enduring human spirit and its capacity for transformation and progress.

As we close the final chapter of this exploration, we leave behind a landscape transformed by the fusion of tradition and technology. It is a landscape where the seeds of tomorrow have been sown, where the values of agriculture have been upheld, and where the potential for a more resilient and prosperous future shines brightly.

In this digital age, agriculture has not only thrived but has also become a beacon of hope and inspiration, demonstrating that innovation and tradition can coexist, sustainability can be achieved, and resilience is within reach. It is a testament to the enduring spirit of the land, the people who tend it, and the communities that depend on it.

10

A Digital Harvest: Looking to the Future of Agriculture

In the hushed moments of twilight, we have reached the final chapter of our journey through the digital age of agriculture. This chapter is a gateway to the future, a glimpse of the possibilities that lie ahead, and a contemplation of the challenges that must be met to ensure the continued prosperity and sustainability of agriculture in the digital era.

The digital age of agriculture is not a static destination but an ever-evolving landscape. The journey we have taken is but a snapshot of a dynamic narrative that continues to unfold. This chapter serves as a launchpad for imagining what agriculture might become and the steps that must be taken to get there.

One of the central themes of this chapter is the boundless potential for innovation. We have seen the transformative power of technology in agriculture, and there is no limit to what can be achieved. From advances in artificial intelligence and biotechnology to the integration of renewable energy sources and the expansion of precision agriculture, the future of farming is ripe with opportunities.

The concept of a circular economy in agriculture is an intriguing vision for the future. It involves a system where resources are used efficiently, waste is minimized, and every component of the agricultural process is recycled and repurposed. This approach not only reduces environmental impact but also opens up new avenues for sustainability and profitability.

The digital age has brought with it a sense of interconnectedness. Farmers, consumers, researchers, policymakers, and innovators are all part of a global ecosystem that can collaborate to address the challenges of agriculture. The digital age of agriculture can be a unifying force, connecting communities, sharing knowledge, and pooling resources to create a more resilient food system.

The integration of blockchain technology into the agricultural supply chain holds the potential for increased transparency, traceability, and trust in the food we consume. With blockchain, consumers can trace the journey of their food from the farm to the table, ensuring that it meets the highest standards of quality and safety.

Education remains a cornerstone for the future of agriculture. Agricultural programs, vocational training, and online courses must continue to evolve to prepare the next generation of farmers, researchers, and agtech innovators for the challenges and opportunities of the digital age.

The agricultural sector also plays a vital role in addressing global challenges. As the world faces issues such as food security, climate change, and resource scarcity, agriculture can be a part of the solution. By implementing sustainable practices, supporting regenerative agriculture, and investing in research, agriculture can contribute to a more resilient and equitable world.

In this chapter, we embrace the complexity and the possibilities that the future holds. The digital age of agriculture is a journey that extends beyond the horizon, where every challenge is an opportunity, every innovation is a stepping stone, and every lesson learned is a catalyst for growth.

As we close this final chapter, we do so with the recognition that the future of agriculture in the digital age is in the hands of those who tend the land, who innovate, who educate, and who collaborate. It is a future where tradition and innovation walk hand in hand, where the values of sustainability and resilience guide the way, and where the harvest of our efforts yields a bountiful and promising tomorrow.

11

Cultivating a Shared Vision: Agriculture's Role in Global Sustainability

As a new day dawns on our journey through the digital age of agriculture, we step into an uncharted territory—a chapter of global importance. In this chapter, we explore the role of agriculture as a linchpin in achieving global sustainability and addressing pressing challenges facing our planet.

Agriculture has always been intertwined with the health and future of our planet. As the human population grows and environmental concerns intensify, agriculture takes center stage as both a driver of change and a solution to global challenges.

One of the key themes of this chapter is the imperative of sustainable agriculture. We delve into how embracing sustainable practices in farming is essential to ensure food security, protect ecosystems, and mitigate climate change. Precision agriculture, organic farming, regenerative agriculture, and other approaches all play a part in this shift towards a more sustainable and harmonious relationship between agriculture and the environment.

As we examine the intricate link between agriculture and climate change, we uncover how the sector both contributes to greenhouse gas emissions and is vulnerable to the consequences of a changing climate. Technology, from carbon sequestration practices to climate-smart agriculture, plays a pivotal role in addressing these challenges.

The concept of circular agriculture comes to the fore in this chapter as well. It involves closing the loop on resource use by recycling waste, maximizing resource efficiency, and minimizing waste generation. Circular agriculture not only conserves resources but also fosters a resilient and adaptable food system.

The digital age has ushered in a new era of transparency and accountability in agriculture. We explore how blockchain technology is being used to trace the origins of food products, creating a more ethical and transparent supply chain. Consumers are increasingly demanding to know where their food comes from and how it was produced, and technology is making this possible.

Global cooperation and knowledge sharing are critical in the pursuit of sustainability. We discuss the role of international organizations, research institutions, and governmental initiatives in addressing global challenges. Collaborative efforts are essential to creating a more equitable and sustainable world.

The United Nations Sustainable Development Goals (SDGs) offer a framework for achieving a more sustainable planet. Agriculture plays a pivotal role in several of these goals, from eradicating hunger and poverty to ensuring access to clean water and sanitation. We explore how agriculture intersects with the SDGs and how achieving them is not only a moral imperative but also an economic one.

In this chapter, we also discuss the importance of resilience in the face of global challenges, such as pandemics, natural disasters, and conflicts.

Agriculture is a lifeline in times of crisis, providing sustenance and stability to communities. We delve into the need for resilient food systems and the role of technology and innovation in achieving this.

As we journey through this chapter, we see that the future of agriculture is inextricably linked to the future of our planet. The digital age has the potential to empower agriculture to be a force for good, a driver of sustainability, and a key actor in addressing the urgent challenges facing humanity.

This chapter is not just a vision of the future; it is a call to action. The path to global sustainability, where agriculture plays a central role, is a journey that requires the collective efforts of individuals, communities, nations, and the global community. It is a future where the fields of innovation, tradition, and sustainability converge to create a world where agriculture nourishes both people and the planet.

12

The Human Element: Nurturing the Soul of Agriculture

As the sun dipped below the horizon and the stars began to twinkle in the night sky, we arrived at the final chapter of our journey through the digital age of agriculture. This chapter explores the enduring, human element of farming—the traditions, the values, and the profound connection between people and the land.

Amidst the technological advancements and global challenges, it is crucial to recognize that the soul of agriculture resides in the hearts and hands of the individuals who tend the soil, nurture the crops, and care for the animals. It is in their stories and experiences that we find the essence of farming in the digital age.

The digital age has brought transformative changes to agriculture, but it has not diminished the significance of traditional wisdom and practices. In this chapter, we delve into the importance of passing down the knowledge of previous generations and preserving the heritage of farming. It is a reminder that technology should complement, not replace, the deep connection to the land and the traditions that have sustained agriculture for centuries.

The relationship between farmers and the land they cultivate is an enduring bond that transcends technology. We explore how sustainable and regenerative practices are rooted in this relationship, how farmers intimately understand the seasons and the soil, and how they work in harmony with nature. Technology augments this understanding but does not replace it.

The concept of "food sovereignty" becomes a focal point in this chapter. It emphasizes the importance of communities having control over their own food systems, ensuring that they can determine their agricultural practices, access to resources, and food security. In the digital age, technology can empower communities to reclaim their food sovereignty, fostering resilience and self-reliance.

We also examine the role of agriculture in cultural identity and heritage. Farming practices, food traditions, and the celebration of local products are a source of pride and a way to preserve and pass down cultural heritage. The digital age offers new opportunities to celebrate and share these traditions on a global scale.

While technology has streamlined many aspects of farming, it has not eliminated the challenges faced by those who work the land. We discuss the importance of supporting and empowering farmers, addressing issues like rural revitalization, access to resources, and economic sustainability. The future of agriculture relies on ensuring that those who tend to the land can do so with dignity and prosperity.

This chapter is a tribute to the farmers who are at the heart of agriculture, who embody the values of hard work, stewardship, and community. It is a celebration of the enduring human spirit, which seeks to nourish the world while respecting the traditions and values that have sustained agriculture for millennia.

As we conclude our journey through the digital age of agriculture, we do so with an acknowledgment that, while technology may be the means, the human element remains the soul of farming. It is a testament to the enduring traditions, values, and the profound connection between people and the land, where innovation and sustainability coexist to create a world where agriculture not only feeds the body but also nourishes the soul.

13

Summary

In our exploration through the digital age of agriculture, we embarked on a journey spanning twelve chapters, each unveiling a different facet of the evolving agricultural landscape. Together, these chapters formed a comprehensive narrative that illuminated the profound transformations, enduring values, and boundless possibilities that define agriculture in the digital era. Here is a summary of our journey:

1. Chapter 1: Agriculture in the Digital Age: Entrepreneurship in Farming
   - Introduced the digital age's impact on agriculture.
   - Explored how technology and innovation are transforming farming.
   - Highlighted the role of farmers as entrepreneurs in this new era.

2. Chapter 2: A New Dawn: The Digital Tools of Agriculture
   - Discussed the wide range of digital tools available to modern farmers.
   - Explored the potential of precision agriculture, IoT, and data-driven decision-making.
   - Emphasized how technology is optimizing farm operations and resource management.

3. Chapter 3: Cultivating Sustainability: Agriculture's Environmental Imperative

- Examined the environmental challenges in agriculture, such as climate change and soil degradation.
- Explored sustainable farming practices and the role of technology in environmental stewardship.
- Showcased innovative approaches to sustainable agriculture, like aquaculture and vertical farming.

4. Chapter 4: The Digital Farmer: Navigating Challenges and Opportunities
   - Explored the evolving role of the "digital farmer."
   - Showcased how farmers are embracing technology and managing the challenges it presents.
   - Discussed the impact of technology on rural communities and rural revitalization.

5. Chapter 5: From Farm to Fork: The Digital Revolution in Food Distribution
   - Highlighted the impact of e-commerce and technology on food distribution.
   - Explored direct-to-consumer sales, online marketplaces, and the role of technology in ensuring food safety and traceability.
   - Emphasized the evolving consumer behavior and the growing demand for transparency in the food supply chain.

6. Chapter 6: Agriculture and the Digital Age: Challenges, Ethical Dilemmas, and the Path Forward
   - Explored the challenges and ethical dilemmas arising from technology in agriculture.
   - Discussed the digital divide, data privacy, and the concentration of power in the tech industry.
   - Advocated for responsible innovation and collaboration to address these challenges.

7. Chapter 7: Seeds of Tomorrow: Education and Innovation in Agricultural

Technology

- Highlighted the importance of education in preparing the next generation for modern farming.
- Showcased the role of innovation and research in agriculture's evolution.
- Discussed the collaboration between traditional and technology-driven approaches in education and innovation.

8. Chapter 8: Nurturing Resilience: Agriculture's Role in a Changing World
- Explored the role of agriculture in addressing global challenges, such as climate change and food security.
- Discussed the importance of sustainable intensification and circular agriculture.
- Advocated for global cooperation and knowledge sharing in building resilience.

9. Chapter 9: Harvesting the Future: Reflections on Agriculture in the Digital Age
- Contemplated the enduring values and traditions in agriculture amidst technological advancements.
- Emphasized the importance of preserving heritage, circular agriculture, and the human connection to the land.
- Advocated for global cooperation in achieving sustainability and addressing global challenges.

10. Chapter 10: A Digital Harvest: Looking to the Future of Agriculture
- Explored the boundless potential for innovation in agriculture.
- Discussed the concept of circular agriculture and the role of technology in achieving sustainability.
- Highlighted the significance of sustainable agriculture and the interplay between global challenges and agriculture.

11. Chapter 11: Cultivating a Shared Vision: Agriculture's Role in Global Sustainability

- Explored the role of agriculture in achieving global sustainability and addressing challenges.
   - Discussed sustainable agriculture, climate change, and circular agriculture.
   - Advocated for food sovereignty, collaboration, and the alignment of agriculture with the United Nations Sustainable Development Goals.

12. Chapter 12: The Human Element: Nurturing the Soul of Agriculture
   - Emphasized the enduring importance of traditional wisdom and practices in agriculture.
   - Explored the connection between farmers and the land and the significance of passing down knowledge.
   - Advocated for preserving cultural heritage, rural revitalization, and the empowerment of farmers.

In this comprehensive journey, we celebrated the remarkable fusion of tradition and technology, sustainability and productivity, and ethics and economics in the digital age of agriculture. It is a reminder that agriculture is not just about food production; it is a complex interplay of values, people, and the land that sustains us. The journey leaves us with a vision of a future where agriculture continues to thrive while honoring its rich heritage and embracing the opportunities of the digital era.

www.ingramcontent.com/pod-product-compliance
Lightning Source LLC
LaVergne TN
LVHW012131070526
838202LV00056B/5955